A Newbies Guide to Android Ice Cream Sandwich

Getting the Most Out of Android
Minute Help Guides

Minute Help Press
www.minutehelp.com

© 2012. All Rights Reserved.

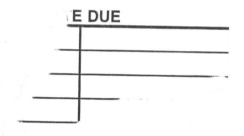

Table of Contents

Part 1: Getting Started

Introduction: Welcome to Android!

We've tried to make this guide simple and easy to read. Along those lines, there are plenty of illustrations and step by step examples for you to follow. We'll help you get your device set up and start to use it. We've also thrown in some tips that will help you start becoming a more powerful Android user right away. We're Android users, too, so we want this guide to give you some information that even advanced users don't know!

However, keep one important thing in mind: Android is not like Apple's IOS or Microsoft's Windows phone. Those two operating systems are controlled by the companies that created them. No one controls Android. Although Google is the company that created and released Android, Android is open source. For those who don't know, open source means that the programming code that makes up the operating system is available for free and can be downloaded from the Internet. Because of this freedom, many wireless carriers and device manufacturers customize Android in various ways to add features that will help distinguish their products in the market place. In other words, the screen that you see on your device may be slightly different from the illustrations here. Don't get worried if that happens. We'll focus on the common features that should be available on any Android device, but try to be flexible as you go through these examples.

How to read this guide

Here are a few conventions that we use in this guide:

Capitalization: We will capitalize the names of parts of Android's user interface. For instance, the main screen you see when you start your device is known as the Home screen, with a capital "H". We'll capitalize the titles of apps, too.

Boldface: We'll use a bold font when we're discussing some part of the user interface that you interact with. When we tell you to touch the **Menu** button, we boldface "Menu".

Menu commands: When you have to go through a series of screens by making a selection to go to the next screen, we'll use common shorthand for this. Instead of saying "press the **Menu button**, touch **Settings**, touch **Wireless & networks**, touch **Wi-Fi settings**, and finally touch **Add Wi-Fi Network**," we'll say "press **Menu**, and select **Settings > Wireless & networks > Wi-Fi settings > Add Wi-Fi Network**".

Now it's time to explore Android!

Chapter 1: Android Basics

One of the first things you will want to do with your smartphone is set up service with a wireless provider. Without entering into an agreement with a wireless carrier -- such as AT&T, Sprint, T-Mobile, or others -- you will not be able to access their wireless networks. All of the major carriers and most of the minor ones offer Android-powered phones to their customers. It's not necessary to enter into a contract, though. Many wireless carriers now even offer powerful Android phones on pay as you go services.

If you ordered a new phone from a wireless carrier, you probably received it ready to go. If you purchased a used phone, you may have to contact your carrier to get a SIM card that you must place in your phone to get wireless service. The specifics of these arrangements will vary from carrier to carrier, as well as manufacturer by manufacturer, so we will not go into more detail about it here. Contact your wireless service for more information.

You may not know that your phone may still be able to access the Internet, even without wireless service. Almost all Android devices are set up to access the Internet over a Wi-Fi network if there is one nearby and you have access to it. For information on how to connect to a Wi-Fi network, see "Connecting to a Wi-Fi network".

Starting up for the first time

When you start your Android device for the first time, after the start up animation, you'll be presented with a screen showing the Android logo. To start setting up your phone, just touch the logo.

Next, the process will give you the opportunity to sign into your Google account. We highly recommend you do so, because this will give you easy access to your contacts, your e-mail, and many other services. If you don't already have a Google account, you have an opportunity here to create one.

You don't have to have a Google account to use your Android device. However, it is difficult to truly take advantage of all of the power of Android unless you are a very advanced user. So we advise you to go ahead and set up an account now.

TIP: If, for some reason, you don't want your device connected to your current Google account, you can just create a new one. That way, you can maintain your privacy but still take advantage of the features Google offers. If you change your mind later, and want to add more previously existing accounts, that's easily done. In fact, we cover it later in this guide.

Now, you will be taken through several steps to help you get your phone set up. Let's go through them, step by step:

Decide if you want to use Google Location services. This service helps determine your physical location from Wi-Fi networks, instead of using GPS. It uses less energy, which tends to strengthen battery life.

If you decide to enable GPS later, you can change it from Settings. We discuss the topic of settings in more detail later.

Next, you'll be asked if you want to use your Google account to backup your phone's data and settings. Select this option. If you are new to smartphones, you may be surprised to find out how quickly you will come to rely on your Android smartphone. Because of this, it's very important to back up your data. This will help you recover your data if the device is lost, damaged, or if you are simply upgrading to a new phone in the future. Google's backup service is not the answer to every problem, but it helps.

Next, the phone will try to detect the current date and time settings from an online network. If your phone can't detect the information, you can enter it yourself.

The Home screen

Finally, you will come to the Home screen. There are three main portions of the screen. Let's take a minute to examine them now.

At the top of the Home screen, you will see a horizontal black bar. There may be several small icons towards the right and left edges of the bar. This is called the Status bar.

Under the Status bar is the large, main portion of the screen. This is what we usually mean when we refer to the Home screen. At the bottom of the screen is another small horizontal bar that contains several icons. These icons represent some of the most common functions you will use on your phone, such as making phone calls or browsing the web. You can launch any of those functions simply by touching the appropriate icon. We'll call this the Favorites bar.

The Home screen is very customizable. You can add widgets, shortcuts to your apps, and even folders so you can easily find your important data and your favorite apps. You can also customize the appearance of your Home screen with wallpaper. To move to other Home screens, simply touch your finger to the screen and swipe it to the left or to the right. When you are using other functions of your Android smartphone, you can usually return to the Home screen at any time by hitting the home icon button at the bottom of your phone.

Chapter 2: Navigating Android

The way you navigate through screens on your Android device may vary widely depending on what type of device you have. For a long time, Google insisted its that all Android device makers include four dedicated navigation buttons on their devices. With the release of their new version of Android -- codenamed Ice Cream Sandwich -- Google has relaxed its position somewhat. However, the buttons can still be found on many devices.

The **Back** button is used to navigate to the last screen you were using. Also, if there is a dialogue window open, or you are using a software keyboard, the back button will close this.

The **Menu** button will show you a set of commands that are specific to the screen where you are currently working. If you are on your Home screen, it will show you menus for the Android OS itself. If you are in an app, you will see commands specific to that app.

You can press the **Home** button any time to return to the Home screen, wherever you are at the moment. If you are on a Home screen to the right or the left of the main Home screen, pressing the Home button returns you to the central Home screen.

If you are on the Home screen, pressing the **Search** button will usually take you to Google search. If you are in an app and that app has a search function built in, the button will take you to that app's search function.

Google does not specifically require a **Search** button, so not all Android devices will feature one. However, it is very common. Most manufacturers will also include a **Power** button and a **Volume** button as well. Some devices may also feature a trackball, which you can use to point at or select a specific element on the screen, just like a computer or a game console.

Usually you will see the buttons we have discussed built into the device, just below the touch screen. However, on some Android devices -- especially tablets -- the buttons may simply be part of the software, and will appear at the bottom of your touchscreen.

How to use the touchscreen

You're probably already familiar with the concept of a touchscreen. Even if you have not used a smartphone before, you have probably already used touch screens at ATMs, grocery store self-checkouts, or other locations. But there is more to the touchscreen than just tapping your selection. There are several types of gestures that your Android device will recognize. Here are some of the most common:

Touch: As you might guess from the name touchscreen, this is the main gesture you will use. To launch an app, simply touch its icon. Touch an icon for a file, and that file will open, using whatever app is associated with that file.

☐ Touch and hold: Generally, if you want to move an object on your screen, you will do so by touching and holding it to select it. Then, you can move the item by dragging it.

☐ Drag: Usually combined with touch and hold–see above. To drag an item on your screen, first touch and hold it. Then, without lifting your finger, drag the item to another location. To move an icon from your main Home screen to another screen, drag it to the left or right edge of the current screen. To delete an item, drag it to the trash.

☐ Swipe: To swipe, touch your finger to the screen and, without lifting it, slide your finger up, down, left, or right. This gesture will cause the contents of your screen to scroll.

☐ Double tap: In many programs, you can rapidly zoom in on some element by touching it twice, rapidly. The element will zoom in or out until it fills the entire screen.

☐ Pinch: To shrink an element on your page, put both your thumb and forefinger on that element and, without lifting, draw them together in a pinching gesture. To make an element larger, making a similar gesture, but spread your fingers further apart.

☐ Rotate the screen: On most Android devices, you can rotate the screen from horizontal to vertical simply by turning your device to the appropriate orientation. You may find that holding the device horizontally works best for reading, but holding it vertically works best for video.

Chapter 3: Alerts, Notifications, and Status Messages

Part of the convenience of an Android device is the fact that it is usually online. Many people use their phones to automatically check their e-mail, social networks, sports results, or investment portfolios on a regular basis. Although it is handy to have this information automatically sent to your phone, you probably don't want to be interrupted every time any event takes place.

The Status bar at the top of your Home screen serves as a place where Android can let you know that changes have taken place, so you can check on them at your convenience.

On the left-hand side of the Status bar, you'll see notifications from apps you have installed. You'll also see notifications from Android itself. On the right-hand side, you'll see a series of icons indicating the status of the phone, plus local time. Additional icons will usually indicate information such as the speed of the network you are using, battery strength, signal strength, time, and more. You'll also see icons indicating such standard cell phone modes as silent, vibrate, alarm, and loudspeaker. The actual appearance of the icons may vary slightly, so check your manual for a full list.

To see what notifications you have in detail and even act on them immediately, if you want, just touch the Notification bar and slide your finger down. If you are interested in a specific notification -- like a certain e-mail you've been waiting for, or a comment on your Facebook page -- just tap that specific notification to be taken to the appropriate app. To close the Notifications screen, tap at the bottom of the panel and slide your finger up, or touch the **Back** button.

Chapter 4: Google Accounts

Part of the point of owning a smartphone is that it gives you a connection to the world, even when you are away from your computer. While an ordinary cell phone will allow you to make calls, a smartphone also gives you access to your contacts, calendars, e-mails, and important documents when you are traveling or are otherwise away from home or work.

If you signed in to your Google account when you first set up your Android phone, you can already access your Gmail messages, Google contacts, and Google calendar using apps that come installed on virtually every Android smartphone. However, you probably have other accounts that you would like to keep track of as well. For instance, many workplaces use Microsoft Exchange to manage e-mails, contacts, and calendars. If you use Microsoft Outlook to access this information at work, this is probably the case for you.

You will probably have to contact your company's tech support desk to get the information you'll need to set up your Android device to access these accounts, but the process is relatively simple.

TIP: you can also use this method to add additional Google accounts, if you have any.

To add additional accounts:

☐ Go to the Home screen.

☐ Press the **Menu** button.

☐ Select **Settings** > **Accounts** > **Sync**.

To add a new account, press the **Add account** button at the bottom of your screen. To edit an existing account, just touch the name of the account you want to edit.

When you press the **Add account** button, you will see a list of many popular communications services that Google supports. Just touch the name of the type of account you want to add.

Enter your username and your password, and your device will be able to access the appropriate account.

If you don't want to sync your entire account to your phone, you can use the E-mail app to just sync additional e-mail accounts. For more information, see "E-mail".

Chapter 5: Opening applications

Opening an app on an Android device is very simple. In most cases, just touch the icon of your app and the app will launch. Much like your computer. you can also open an app by opening a document that you would normally view with that app.

There are probably icons for a few apps already on your Home screen. supplied by your smartphone manufacturer. To find any other apps that you have installed you'll need to use the Launcher. There will be a small icon in your Favorites bar, at the bottom of your Home screen. that looks like a series of small squares, arranged in a grid. Tap that to open the Launcher.

As we've already discussed, there are slight differences between the versions of Android that you may find on different devices. For instance, there are a few different Launcher programs available. Yours may look different than the one pictured here, but it will operate in a very similar way.

Your Launcher shows icons for virtually every app installed on your device. Generally, the icons will be shown in alphabetical order, by app name. Some Launchers may give you options to view the icons with different views as well. If you have too many apps for the Launcher to fit on one screen, you can scroll to see the additional apps by swiping your finger. To quickly return to apps that you have recently used, touch and hold the Home button.

       ☐   A window will appear that shows an image of apps you've recently used.

       ☐   Touch the appropriate icon to launch that app or, to exit, hit the **Back** button

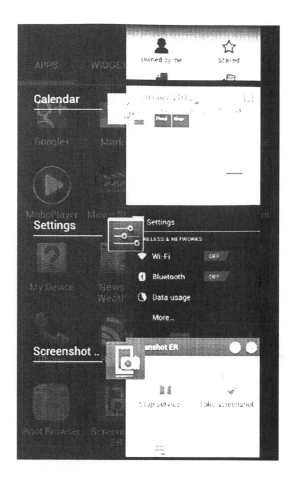

TIP: Unlike the iPhone, Android offers true multitasking. This means that you can have more than one app open at a time, and every app will continue to run. In other words, if you are loading a large webpage or browser, and you open your Facebook app to update your status, the browser will continue to load the page.

This can be very convenient, but beware. If you suddenly switch from one app to another make sure the old app is truly closed when you are done. One the way to be sure you have totally closed the app is to use the **Back** button until it returns you to your Home screen.

Chapter 6: Entering data

Because Android devices are generally small, one of the biggest challenges in using such a device is entering data. When you are trying to enter text in an e-mail, text message or tweet, that small screen can present a challenge.

Some Android smartphones have a built-in keyboard. If so, you will use that to enter text. If not, your Android device will offer you a software keyboard that only appears on the screen when you need it.

Also, you can control many functions of your device simply by speaking. Let's explore some of the options for inputing data and commands to your Android phone.

If you don't have a built-in keyboard, the Android OS will supply a software keyboard when you need to enter text. To save screen space, the keyboard only appears when you tap in a field where you can enter data -- like the body of an e-mail, or a text field on a web page form you're filling out. The onscreen keyboard works much like a traditional typewriter-style keyboard, featuring numbers, letters and function keys such as **Shift**, **Delete** and **Enter**.

It also has a convenient feature to speed up your typing on many commonly used words. As you type, a small strip will appear along the top of the keyboard that shows words in Android's dictionary that begin with the letters you type. When you see the word you want, just tap on it to insert that word into your text.

Some Android devices also include an app called Swype. Swype modifies your keyboard on the screen with a feature that some people find speeds up their typing. With Swype, instead of touching each key for every letter in the word, start by touching your finger down on the first letter you want, and drag it across every key in the word you want to type.

You may find that Swype works better for you, and there are other keyboard replacement apps available. You may want to experiment a little to see what option is best for you.

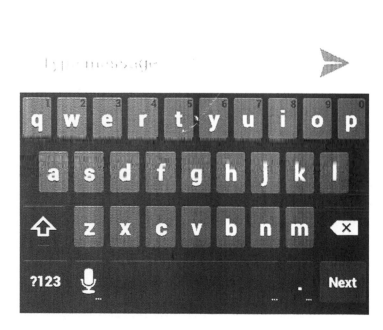

Since Android devices are smartphones, logically, these devices already have built-in microphones. It would certainly be convenient, in many circumstances, to be able to issue commands using your voice. Fortunately, the good folks at Google thought of that too, and this option is available.

To turn voice input on:

☐ Go to Home screen.

☐ Press the **Menu** button.

☐ Go to **Settings > Language & keyboard > Android keyboard > Voice input**.

☐ Now, whenever you see the microphone icon on your screen, just touch it to select voice input.

☐ When prompted to speak, say the command you want Android to execute, or the text you wish to enter.

TIP: You can also speak common punctuation such as "comma", "period", or "exclamation point".

One of the biggest challenges you will encounter when trying to enter text is editing. Because the screen is so small, it is hard to put the cursor exactly where you want it. When you tap in a text field that already has text in it, the cursor will appear there. However, to make editing easier, just follow these simple steps.

To edit text:

☐ Tap in a text field, near where you want the cursor to appear.

Android will place the cursor where you tapped, and a blue tab will appear, and briefly remain, at the bottom of the cursor.

If the cursor is not exactly where you wanted it to be, just touch the blue tab and slide your finger to the appropriate location.

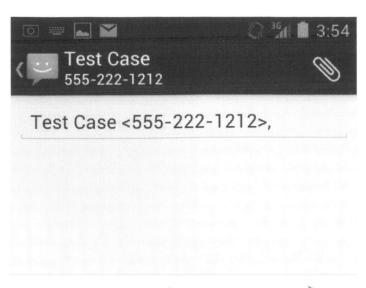

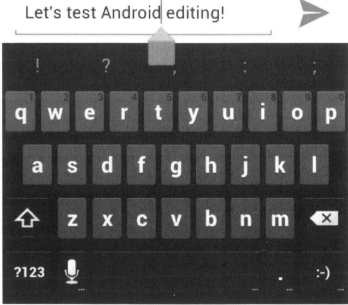

☐   To select text, touch and hold a word. A menu at the top of the screen will allow you to select all, copy or cut.

☐   If you chose only one word, a cursor with a blue tab will appear at the beginning and end of that word. To expand the selection area, simply touch one or both of the tabs and drag it.

Test Case <555-222-1212>,

If you want to replace that text with new text, simply type as usual.

To copy, cut or paste text, touch anywhere in the selected area and hold your finger down. Using the icons at the top of the touchscreen, select which function you want to use.

Part 2: Using Android to communicate

Chapter 1: Connection Settings

One of the keys to enjoying your Android smartphone is connectivity. Using this small, hand-held device, you can connect to wireless networks, Wi-Fi, your computer, and Bluetooth accessories. The more devices you can connect to, the more convenient your Android phone will be.

As already discussed, you will have to make arrangements directly with your wireless carrier to access their networks. The exact details of how you will connect will vary, depending on which Android device you have, and which carrier you use.

Connecting to Bluetooth devices

Connecting to Bluetooth devices, such as a hands-free headset for driving, is easy. You can set your Android device to automatically scan for Bluetooth devices.

To connect to a Bluetooth device:

On on your Home screen.

Press **Menu** button.

Select **System settings > Wireless & networks > Bluetooth settings**.

TIP: Android OS supplies a name for your device as a default identifier, but you may want to replace that with something easier to remember. To change the name, go to **Settings > Wireless & networks > Bluetooth settings**, where you can edit the name of your device.

TIP: Your Bluetooth device may be password protected. Check the manufacturers information to see if a password has been set. If you can't find the information try "0000" or "1234". Manufacturers often use these as default.

If you know you are no longer going to be using a Bluetooth device that you have paired to your phone, you can delete that profile.

To delete the profile for a Bluetooth device:

>Go to your Home screen.

>Press **Menu** button.

>Select **Settings > Wireless & networks > Bluetooth settings**.

>Touch the name of the device you want to delete, and hold that name until the pop-up menu appears. Select **Unpair**.

Connecting to Wi-Fi networks

With your Android phone, you will frequently have two main options for connecting to the Internet. Obviously, you can use your connection through the wireless carrier. However, most Android devices can also access the Internet from a Wi-Fi network, if you have access to that network.

This is important because your plan may have limits on the amount of data you can use. Generally, going over those limits becomes very expensive, very quickly. Using Wi-Fi, you can frequently access the Internet from your home, your office, the coffee shop, or airport, without using additional data through your wireless service plan.

If there is an open Wi-Fi network nearby, you can connect using the following steps:

☐ Go to Home screen.

☐ Press **Menu** button.

☐ Select **Settings > Wireless & networks >Wi-Fi**.

☐ Touch **Wi-Fi**.

☐ If Wi-Fi is not on, turn it on.

☐ The device will show a list of networks it detects.

☐ Touch the name of the network you want to join.

☐ If the network is password protected, your device will pop up a dialog box where you can enter password.

TIP: Much like Bluetooth networks, if you later wish to remove a Wi-Fi network from your list, just touch and hold the name of the network, and choose **Forget network**.

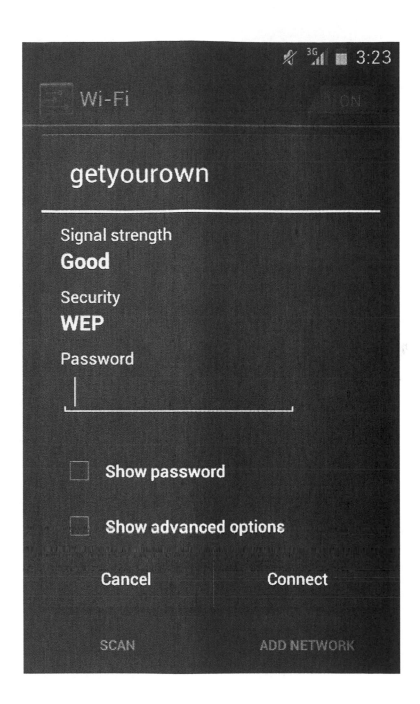

Wi-Fi ON

getyourown

Signal strength
Good

Security
WEP

Password

☐ Show password

☐ Show advanced options

Cancel   Connect

SCAN   ADD NETWORK

Connecting to your computer and sharing your wireless connection

Sometimes, the fastest and simplest way to get data from your computer to your Android device is simply to connect the two with a USB cable:

☐   Take a standard USB cable.

☐   Plug the large connector into your computer.

☐   Plug the small connector into your file.

☐   Your phone will usually display a screen showing that your device is connected.

☐   Press the button that says **Turn on USB storage**.

☐   If you don't see this screen, pull down the notifications screen and select the notification that says **USB connected**.

TIP: when you are using USB connectivity, your computer sees your Android device as just another storage device -- like an external hard drive, or a USB drive. Just as in those cases, make sure to follow your computer's normal procedures to unmount the device before you disconnect it.

Sharing your Internet connection

One particularly useful feature of Android devices is their ability to share their Internet connection with other devices, such as laptop computers. This is sometimes referred to as tethering. You can share your wireless connection with other devices that you connect to with a USB cable, or using Bluetooth. Or, you can simply opt to turn your device into a portable WiFi hotspot, and share your connection with any WiFi enabled device.

To tether your device via USB:

☐   Use a USB cable to connect your phone to your computer.

☐   A USB icon appears in the Notifications bar. You'll see either the notification **Connected as a media device** or **Connected as a camera** on the Notifications screen.

☐   Navigate to **Settings > Wireless & networks > More > Tethering & portable hotspot**.

☐   If **USB tethering**, is not selected, check it.

To tether your device via Bluetooth:

☐   Pair your phone with your computer, using the instructions previously given.

☐   Set your computer to connect to the Internet via Bluetooth.

☐   Navigate to **Settings > Wireless & networks > More > Tethering & portable hotspot**.

If **Bluetooth tethering**, is not selected, check it.

To stop sharing your data connection, uncheck **Bluetooth tethering**.

To share your WiFi connection as a hotspot:

Navigate to **Settings > Wireless & networks > More > Tethering & portable hotspot**.

If **Portable Wi-Fi hotspot**, is not selected, check it.

When the phone starts broadcasting its Wi-Fi network name connect to it from your computer.

To stop sharing your data connection, uncheck **Portable Wi-Fi hotspot**.

TIP: Check with your wireless carrier before tethering devices to your smartphone. This may not be allowed under your service contract, and it could cause your carrier to drop you. Better safe than sorry!

In addition, if your workplace has a virtual private network, you may also be able to access that from your Android smartphone. However, you will have to contact your tech support specialists for more information.

Chapter 2: Browsing the Web and Checking Email

If you have used web browsers on computers, you'll find the experience is very similar on your Android smartphone. Access your browser by touching the Browser icon in your Favorites bar (the one that looks like a tiny globe of Earth). It will launch and take you to your home page. If your smartphone manufacturer has some sort of Internet portal, that may be your default setting. Usually, the default setting will be Google.

To search for a site, tap the search box and type in the site name or phrase you want to search for. To enter a specific web address, tap in the Address bar at the top of the screen.

That's not the only way your Android phone takes advantage of the versatility of the World Wide Web. Many apps also use web browser-like technology in their apps as an easy way for your phone to send and receive data. But the most important thing to know is that your Android web browser offers pretty much every feature you're used to from your computer, only smaller. Android devices even support Adobe's popular Flash technology for web videos and games -- something your friends with iPhones can't say.

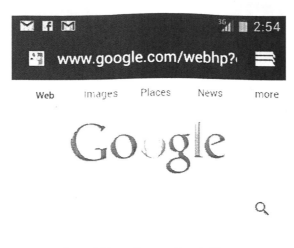

Location unavailable - update

TIP: Also keep in mind that you don't have to use the browser that comes installed on your Android device. You can download Android versions of the popular Firefox, Chrome and Opera browsers, which comes in handy if you use one of those browsers on another machine and want to sync your bookmarks, or other data, between the two devices. Additionally, there are companies that specialize in Android browsers, such as Dolphin and Skyfire. We'll discuss good places to find and download apps in just a few pages.

E-mail

If you followed our advice earlier and signed in to your Google account when you set up Android, your phone is already automatically configured to allow you to easily access your Gmail. However, you probably have other e-mail addresses -- from work, school or other organizations -- that you'd like to access. You can easily do that with Android's Email app.

Using Email, it's easy to set up your Android phone to access your other e-mail accounts. Just follow these steps:

☐   Touch the icon of your Email app to launch Email.

☐   Enter your e-mail account and your password.

In most cases, that's it. Email will be smart enough to know how to access most types of e-mail accounts with just this information.

TIP: in the future, if you want to add additional accounts, simply open your Email app, press the **Menu** button, select settings, and touch **Add account**.

If you work in an office where you use Microsoft Outlook to manage your e-mails, contacts, and calendar, you will probably be able to set up your Android phone to access those accounts as well. You will have to contact your organization's IT department for more information, however.

Account setup

You can set up email for most
accounts in just a few steps.

email address

Password

Send email from this account by
default.

Chapter 3: Text Messaging and Making Calls

Let's face it, some folks just love text messages. It's certainly a convenient way for a group of people to communicate amongst themselves quickly and easily. But even if you are usually not a text message user, you may find yourself using it more often with your Android smart phone. Android's Messaging app makes it easy for a group of people to communicate using cell phones, computers, or smart phones.

To launch Messaging, touch the Messaging icon.

    ☐   Any messages you have received will be displayed on the screen.

    ☐   If you want to send a new text message, touch **New message**.

    ☐   To attach a file, touch the **Menu** button and select **Attach**.

TIP: if you get a notification from Android that you have a new text message, you can quickly reply by pulling down the Notifications screen and touching the appropriate notification.

Test Case <555-222-1212>,

Let's test Android editing!

Making calls

You can do so many things with your Android phone, it can be easy to get caught up and forget about the basics. You can use your Android smart phone like a conventional cell phone if you want, but Android offers several features that you may find very convenient.

Any good cellphone allows you to create a list of contacts, to easily get in touch with the people you call most often. Android takes that concept to a whole new level. Using Android's People app, you can coordinate all the information you have on each contact, and use every method available to get in touch with them.

You can store photos of your contacts, phone numbers, addresses, social media handles, e-mail addresses and more. When you need to communicate with a group -- to collaborate on a project, or arrange a get-together, you can create lists, or groups, or filter your contacts through specific criteria.

Your own contact information is also stored in a profile called "Me", making it easier to share any of your information with friends and colleagues. You can view all of your contacts in the People app. You can also create Lists of contacts that have features in common, like coworkers or Google+ friends, for easy communication. Anywhere you see the photo of one of your contacts, you can tap it to open the contact's page in People.

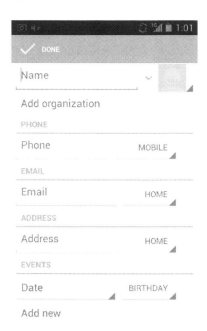

You can also create a shortcut for a specific contact and place that on your Home screen by following these simple steps:

Go to the Home screen where you want to place a Contact.

Open the Launcher.

Choose the **Widgets** tab and scroll until you reach the Contacts icon.

Touch and hold the icon.

A small image of the Home screen you have chosen will appear.

Drag the Contact to the location on the Home screen where you want it to display, and let go.

The People app will open

Select the contact you want to use

You can also make phone calls from the Phone app, either by dialing a number or by selecting a number from Call Log. Finally, you can place a phone call from your contacts.

TIP: if you want to temporarily disable all phone calls, press and hold the **Power** button and touch the Menu item that says **Airplane mode.**

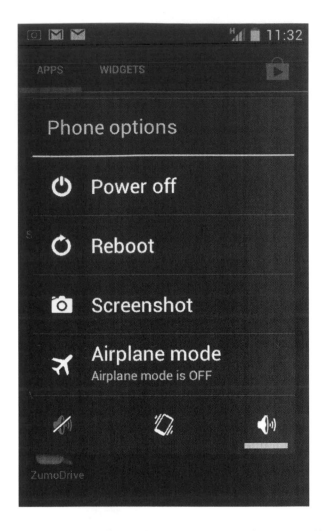

When you get a phone call, Android will use caller ID to display the incoming phone number on your screen, if it is available. Under that number, you'll see an icon of a telephone. Drag the icon to the right to answer the phone call. Drag it to the left to decline the call, and send it to voicemail.

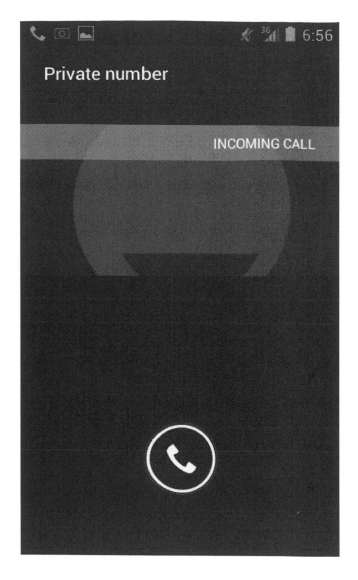

If you want to redial a number that you recently dialed, or call back a number that recently called you, you can do so from the Call Log:

☐   Touch the Phone icon.

☐   Touch the Call Log icon at the top of your screen.

☐   Simply touch any phone number there to call it.

TIP: to add a phone number to your contacts from your Call Log, simply touch and hold that entry. When the pop-up menu appears, touch **Add to contact**.

Calling anyone already listed in your contacts is also easy:

☐   Touch the People icon to launch the People app. You can also access contacts from your Phone app.

☐   Drag your finger up or down to scroll to the contact you want.

☐   To call that contact, touch the name.

When you are on a phone call, the screen on your Android device shows a series of buttons for common tasks such as hanging up, mute, or adding another number to the phone call.

Voice Actions

You can also place a call by simply speaking to your phone, if you have Google voice typing activated. To activate it:

Go to your Home screen.

Touch the **Menu** button.

Select **System settings > Language & input**.

Select **Google voice typing**.

TIP: Google voice typing requires that your Android smartphone access Google's huge library of human speech data, so it only works if you have an active wireless or Wi-Fi connection.

You can issue commands such as "call" followed by the name of any contact in your Google People app. You can also say "call" and speak the number you want to dial.

TIP: To get driving directions, Android also understands phrases like "go to" followed by a spoken address. You can also use voice recognition to perform tasks such as sending a text message.

Voicemail

When a caller leaves you a voicemail message, Android will send a notification to your Notification bar to listen to your voicemail:

☐   Open the notifications panel

☐   Touch your voicemail notification.

Your actual voicemail service will be provided to you by your wireless carrier, so you'll have to contact them for instructions on how to initially set up voicemail.

TIP: On a normal cell phone you have to go through your voicemails one by one, in the order of most recently received. With your smart phone, there are apps available that will visually show what voicemails you have waiting, so you can tackle the most important ones first. Google offers a free app called Google Voice, which we will discuss later. Additionally, there are other alternatives to explore at the Google Play app market.

Part 3: Making Your Phone Smart

Chapter 1: Managing applications

When you first get your Android smart phone, it will probably have very few apps on it, and lots of room for storage. However, as time goes by and you add more apps, data, and media, managing your apps becomes very important.

Additionally, it's a good idea to know more about how your apps work. For instance, if you find that you have added several new apps, and your phone is not behaving properly -- crashing, operating slowly -- you'll probably want to identify what app, or apps, are causing the problem, so you can get rid of them.

How to manage your apps

If you are certain that you want to remove a specific app, that's easily done. Just follow these simple instructions:

☐ Open your Launcher.

☐ Scroll until you see the icon for the app you want to remove.

☐ Touch and hold the icon of the app you want to remove. When the screen pops up to allow you to move or uninstall the app, drag the icon to the trashcan.

If you'd like to get more information about the app before you choose to delete it, follow these steps:

☐ Go to your Home screen.

☐ Press the **Menu** button.

☐ Touch **Manage apps**.

On the apps screen you'll see three tabs at the top of your screen. You can see all of the apps you've downloaded, just those apps still installed on your internal storage device, or only apps that are currently running. At the bottom of the screen you'll also see a graph that indicates how much memory is being used and how much memory remains.

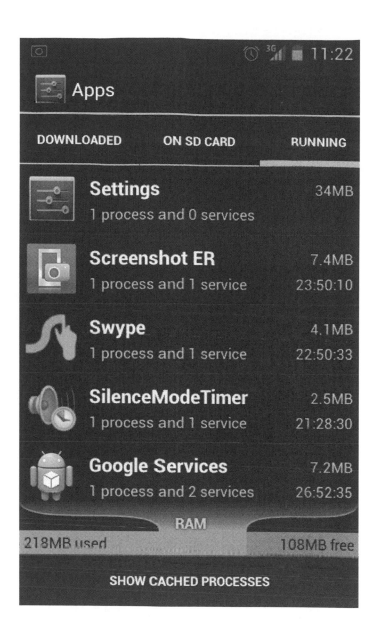

Apps

DOWNLOADED	ON SD CARD	RUNNING

Settings — 34MB
1 process and 0 services

Screenshot ER — 7.4MB
1 process and 1 service — 23:50:10

Swype — 4.1MB
1 process and 1 service — 22:50:33

SilenceModeTimer — 2.5MB
1 process and 1 service — 21:28:30

Google Services — 7.2MB
1 process and 2 services — 26:52:35

RAM

218MB used — 108MB free

SHOW CACHED PROCESSES

To see more detail about an app, just touch that app's name and you'll be taken to a detailed screen that will show you how much storage that specific app takes up, and what other functions of your Android device the app can affect. These are known as permissions. On this screen you can find valuable information that may indicate whether or not an app is creating conflicts. If an app is currently running, you can stop it by pressing the **Force stop** button. You can also remove the app entirely by pressing **Uninstall**.

Additionally, there are times when you may want to erase your internal storage completely. For instance, if you purchase a new card with more storage, you'll want to put that in your Android smartphone, and perhaps want to move the old card to another device. Here's how to do it:

☐ Go to your Home screen.

☐ Press the **Menu** button.

☐ Select **System Settings** › **Storage**.

☐ Scroll to the bottom of the screen and touch **Erase SD card**.

TIP: Remember, before you remove your SD card, to go to the storage screen and touch **Unmount SD card**.

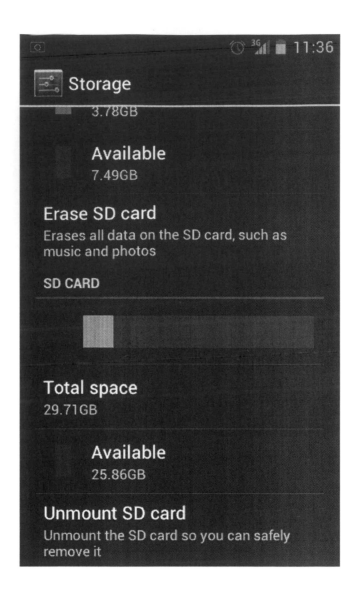

Storage

3.78GB

Available
7.49GB

Erase SD card
Erases all data on the SD card, such as music and photos

SD CARD

Total space
29.71GB

Available
25.86GB

Unmount SD card
Unmount the SD card so you can safely remove it

Chapter 2: Customizing Android

The simplest way to customize your Android device is just to add and remove apps. Each app adds specialized functions to your Android phone, and enables you to easily access the power and flexibility of your smartphone.

However, there are several other things you can do to change the appearance of your Android device and the way it works to make it better suit your needs and your mood.

TIP: Keep in mind that there is almost no limit to the amount of customization that you can do with your Android device. Although these techniques are not for beginners, it's worth it to know that taking full control over your phone -- including modifying, upgrading, or even deleting the entire Android operating system -- can be as simple as installing an app. You're in control, not your wireless carrier, or the device manufacturer.

For now, however, we'll focus on simpler techniques.

The background image you see on your Home screen is called a wallpaper. Many people keep a few different wallpapers on their phone, and change them whenever the mood suits them. Here's how to change your wallpaper:

    ☐   Go to your Home screen.

    ☐   Touch the **Menu** button.

    ☐   Touch **Wallpaper**.

A pop-up menu will appear that says **Choose wallpaper from**. You can select **Gallery**, **Live Wallpapers**, or standard **Wallpapers**. To use a photo that you have taken yourself, choose Gallery.

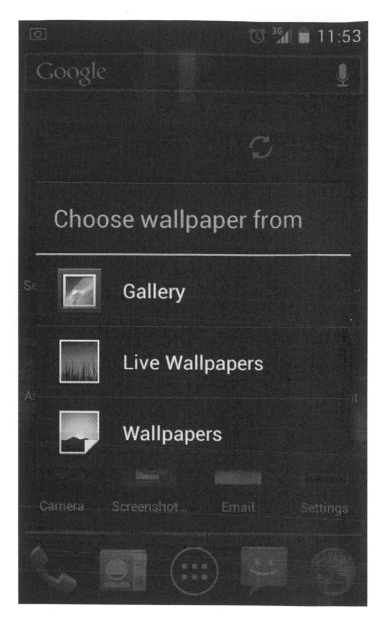

Live wallpapers are basically small apps that run in the background. Live wallpapers simply offer some basic animation that creates movement in the background that is eye-catching and attractive. Some Live Wallpapers even update with useful information such as the time or the weather.

You can download and install live wallpapers from many of the same popular sources where you get your Android apps. We'll discuss these sources in more detail in just a few pages.

Additionally, keep in mind that you have control over what apps and widgets appear on your Home screen, and where they appear as well. To increase your efficiency and your enjoyment, try placing the icons of the apps you use most frequently on your main Home screen for easy access. Place the icons of apps you want to access easily, but don't use all the time, on the additional Home screen pages to the left or right of the main Home screen.

Also, you are probably familiar with the concept of apps, but you may not be as familiar with the concept of a widget. A widget is an icon that is connected to a particular app, but it offers just a handful of features you might need quickly. For instance, if you update Twitter frequently, you might want to put a widget on your Home screen that specifically allows you to enter your tweets and see the latest tweets you have received immediately -- without going to your Launcher or even opening your Twitter app.

To place an app or a widget on your home page:

☐   Go to the Home screen where you want the new icon to go.

☐   Open the Launcher.

☐   Choose either the **Apps** tab or the **Widgets** tab and scroll until you reach the item you want.

☐   Touch and hold the icon you have chosen.

☐   A small image of the Home screen you have chosen will appear.

☐ Drag the icon of the app or widget you have chosen to the location on the Home screen where you want it to display, and let go.

TIP: Remember, you can add contacts you use frequently to your Home screen as well. For a reminder of how to do this, see "Using Contacts."

Chapter 3: Preinstalled Google apps

As the creator of Android, Google offers a variety of free apps that provide a host of useful functions. It's usually the case that your device manufacturer will include several of these on your Android device. You can learn what some of those apps are, and what they do, below:

Google Search

You can search the web, your contacts, your apps, or all three.

Google Maps

Search for specific locations, call up area maps and get directions.

Gmail

Use your Gmail account on your Android phone

Google Calendar

Automatically sync your Google Calendar is to your phone.

Google Contacts

Syncs your Google contacts to your phone.

These Google apps may be included on your Android device as well, or can be downloaded directly from Google Play:

YouTube

Watch videos or upload videos you take from your phone.

Latitude

See your friends' locations on a map.

Goggles

This clever app uses pictures to search the web. Take a photo of landmarks around you and get more information about the area where you are.

Google Voice

Control where your calls are routed, what messages your callers receive and manage your voicemail. Also make Internet phone calls at low rates.

Google Talk

Send instant messages through Google's chat service.

Google+

Easily use Google's new social networking service

Google Finance

Syncs information on your portfolio from your Google Finance account.

Google Shopper

Search for deals with this app that searches for the lowest price on specific products.

Google Earth

Learn information and view maps about any area.

Blogger

Publish blog posts for this popular, Google-owned blogging service.

Google Translate

This app can translate 15 languages as spoken words and more than 50 as text.

Google Offers

This daily deal site offers local discounts, based on your location.

My Tracks

Record and share your workout stats as you run, bike, or hike.

Chapter 4: Apps Galore

Google Play

Google Play, formerly known as Android market, is the online store developed by Google to sell apps. You can also purchase electronic media such as music, videos, and e-books.

However, keep in mind that Android is an open system, as we discussed before. Unlike Apple's iPhone, you don't have to get your apps from Google Play. Any file with an ".apk" extension is probably an installer that can installed as an app on your Android device.

Just like a computer, having a variety of sources for your apps gives you flexibility and control, but also creates problems. Like your computer, you will want to make certain only to install software from sources you trust. Some software may contain malware or viruses. Additionally, if you pay for your new app with your credit card, you must also be concerned about the security of the transaction.

This is one of the reasons you'll probably want to get to know Google Play. First of all, if you signed in to your Google account when you set up your Android phone, you already have a Google Play account. Secondly, all purchases through Google Play are processed by Google, so you can have some reasonable expectation of security.

Finally, Google does attempt to ensure that no harmful apps are distributed through Google Play. Keep in mind, Google does not examine every app the way Apple does for its App Store. Anyone can add an app to Google Play. Google simply attempts to remove any app with highly negative reviews. When you're starting out with your Android smartphone, it will probably be better to stick with apps that have been around for a long time, have excellent reviews, and many satisfied users.

To go to Google Play:

☐   Touch the icon for Launcher.

☐   Touch Google Play.

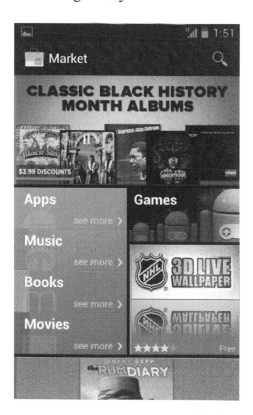

There are too many apps out there for us to give you any type of complete listing, and new apps are added every day. However, to get you started, here is a listing of several different types of apps you may want to use.

Social networking

Most major social networking sites, including Facebook, Twitter, Linked In, FourSquare, and Google+, offer free apps that you can get from a variety of sources. If you are an active social networker, there are also plenty of paid apps with features for extra productivity. Many blogging platforms like Blogger, WordPress, and LiveJournal, also have apps.

Video

All major broadcast TV networks have free apps that allow you to view schedules, special features, excerpts, and sometimes entire episodes of their TV shows. Many cable TV networks offer such apps as well. Depending on the region in which you live, your cable TV provider may offer on-demand video through an app as well. Finally, specialized Internet video-on-demand services such as Amazon Prime, Hulu, Netflix and YouTube have apps that you can download.

File syncing

If you travel frequently, or collaborate with colleagues, it can be very handy to always have up-to-date versions of your files with you. Google and Amazon are two major companies offering free apps to help you synchronize data in the cloud. There are also free options from several companies specializing in cloud sync, like Box, Dropbox, and SugarSync.

Music

Google and Amazon both offer free Android apps that allow you to upload your music collection to the cloud, so you can listen to it anywhere. Additionally, apps like Pandora, Spotify, and Rdio offer apps that allow you to create playlists from their vast music catalogs. Finally, you can store your music directly on your Android device, so you can listen even when you don't have an Internet connection.

Online banking

Virtually all major national banks, many regional banks, and even some local banks offer apps that allow you to handle some transactions online, security. PayPal offers a free app if you have a PayPal account. Insurance companies and financial service firms have also begun to allow you to access your account through Android apps as well.

Games

Android devices make great handheld game-playing devices. You'll find many popular casual games available for free, such as Angry Birds. You can also buy sophisticated versions of popular computer games and console games, such as Dead Space or Need for Speed.

TIP: There are other sources of Android apps besides Google Play. Unlike Apple, Google does not control this market. Since the success of Amazon's Android-based Kindle Fire tablet, Amazon's app store has become very popular. Opera, the web browser developer, also has a store. Many independent marketplaces also exist, such as Mobihand and GetJar.

Chapter 5: Camera

Most Android devices include a camera. These vary widely from device to device, so check your manufacturer's information for specifics. However, the controls of the camera are usually handled by the Android software, so those are fairly standardized from device to device. Usually your camera will be able to take both photos and video.

To access your camera:

☐   Go to the Launcher.

☐   Touch the Camera icon.

☐   You'll see something like the screen shown below:

Use the large area on your left as your viewfinder. If you want to use a specific part of the viewfinder image as a focus point -- someone's face, for example -- just touch that part of the screen.

The icons that you see on the right side of the viewfinder give you the following capabilities:

☐ Mode: Switch between camera, video, and panorama modes. Panorama allows you to easily take several photos of scenes and then tie them together into a bigger picture.

☐ Switch: Most Android phones allow you to hold the phone with the screen facing you (front-facing) or, if you'd prefer, to turn it around and look through the more traditional viewfinder (rear-facing). Toggle between these modes with the Camera icon.

☐ Zoom: Touch & hold, then slide to zoom in and out.

☐ Settings: Allows you to manually adjust the automatic color and light settings for your picture, and more.

After taking a picture or video, you can go to the Gallery app to share it quickly by e-mail, text message, Twitter, Facebook, Bluetooth, and more.

You use the Gallery app to view and share your photos and videos. These can be photos and videos you take with the built-in camera in your Android device, or photos and videos that you download, or that people send to you. To open the Gallery, simply touch its icon in the Launcher. Also, you can enter the Gallery from the Camera app.

To enter the Gallery from Camera:

☐ On the upper right-hand corner of the touchscreen viewfinder, you can see a thumbnail of the most recent picture you've taken. Touch the thumbnail.

☐ The picture opens in a larger version, in the viewfinder area.

☐ Touch the Gallery icon to go to the Gallery.

☐ You will also see options to share with social networking accounts you have set up, and photo editing apps you may have installed.

In the Gallery, you will see a screen full of small thumbnails of images you have taken or downloaded -- helping you quickly identify albums you have set up. Gallery automatically creates a few albums that you might want, like Downloads and Camera. You can delete any of these albums if you don't want them by touching and holding that album. Android will select it and offer you a menu of options.

Touch the icon for an album to see thumbnails of all of the photos in that album. Touch any thumbnail to see a larger version of the photo.

Touch and hold an album or photo to share it using any of the accounts you have set up previously.

Share photos just by touching

The newest version of Android brings a feature that can be very helpful in a wireless, multimedia world. If your Android smartphone is equipped to use Near Field Communications (NFC), you can quickly share your photos or other media with another Android NFC user, just by touching the two devices together. NFC is a short-range wireless connection, a little like Bluetooth.

To share photos via NFC:

☐   Make sure both devices have NFC turned on.

☐   Open a photo you'd like to share.

☐   Move the back of your phone toward the back of the other device.

☐   When the devices connect, you see the message **Touch to beam**.

☐   Touch your screen to send the image.

Chapter 6: Optimizing Battery Life

In some ways your Android device is as powerful and sophisticated as your computer. However, because your Android device is much smaller, its battery is smaller, too. One of the keys to enjoying your Android device is optimizing battery life.

Check your battery strength by going to **System settings > Battery**.

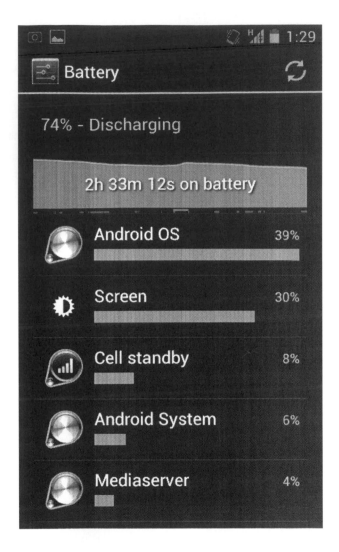

If an app is using a great deal of power, and it is not an app you absolutely need, you may want to uninstall it. To uninstall an app:

☐ Touch the app's name.

☐ You will be taken to a screen where you can uninstall that app.

☐ Touch the **Application info** button.

Chapter 7: Security

Security is one of the most important issues you will face on your Android device. The longer you have your Android phone, and the more you use it, the more sensitive information will be stored on your phone. If your phone is ever lost or stolen, someone may have enough information to attempt identity theft. At the very least, it can be difficult re-creating all that information on a new device.

Some folks are reluctant to think about good security practice. They are concerned that extra security means less ease of use. But that doesn't have to be the case. There are several simple steps you can take that will greatly increase your security, but are easy to do.

First, set a screen lock. You can set your phone to automatically lock the screen after a certain amount of time passes, preventing anyone who does not know the unlock code from using it. It's a good idea to set one right away.

To set a screen lock:

☐ Go to your Home screen

☐ Touch the **Menu** button

☐ Select **System settings > Security > Screen lock**.

☐ You can choose **None, Slide, Face Unlock, Pattern, PIN** or **Password**. These selections range, in order, from least secure to most secure.

☐ If you selected Password or PIN, set your unlock code.

☐ Choosing Pattern will show you a pattern of nine dots in a three-by-three square. Set your finger down on a dot and, without lifting your finger, draw a line through additional dots, creating a pattern. You will use that pattern to unlock your phone.

TIP: At first, select the **Use visible pattern** option in Settings. Android will draw a line on your screen as your finger moves, making it easier to see the pattern you are drawing.

Don't worry too much that you may forget your unlock code. If you fail to unlock your phone a certain amount of times -- usually three -- you will be locked out, but you can use your Google account to reset your password.

Only download apps from trusted software. We've already discussed various sources where you can find apps. Unless you are dealing with an established software developer, a widely used app, and a highly satisfied user base, be extremely cautious about installing any app. Do your research!

Finally, consider adding security apps. We honestly only recommend this if you feel you have unusually high security requirements. Some security apps can be expensive and, no matter how good the app is, no security is perfect. The first two steps we've already discussed will be enough for many people -- plus backing up your account and app data, as discussed earlier in this guide.

Fortunately, many security apps offer a free version, with limited features. Try these first and, if you feel you need more advanced features, you can buy the app.

TIP: Remember the instructions on how to check the amount of storage your app is using, the amount of energy it is using and the amount of memory it uses. Monitoring that data can help you tell if you have a malicious or buggy app.

Chapter 8: Settings

There are two levels of settings on your Android phone. There are Android's system settings that affect the operation of your entire device, and most individual apps have settings as well, that only affect that app.

You can save a lot of frustration by remembering that system settings always take precedence -- if you turn off Wi-Fi in your Android device, then no app will be able to use Wi-Fi, even if the settings indicate that it should.

To access the settings for a specific app:

☐ Open the app from Launcher.

☐ Touch the **Menu** button.

To access Android settings:

☐ Go to your Home screen

☐ Press the **Menu** button.

☐ Touch **System settings**.

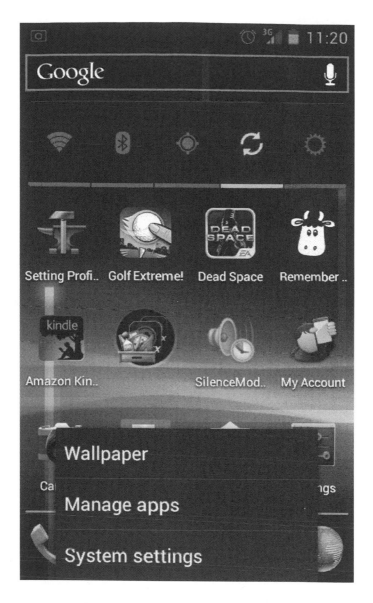

Usually, you won't need to make many changes to these settings --
the defaults are generally good enough when you first start using
your Android phone. However, we urge you to glance at some of
these screens to get a better idea of what kinds of options you can
easily control.

- Wi-Fi

- Bluetooth

- Data usage

- Sound

- Display

- Storage

- Battery

- Apps

- Accounts & sync

- Location services

- Security

- Language & input

- Backup & rest

- Date & time

- Accessibility

- Developer options

- About phone

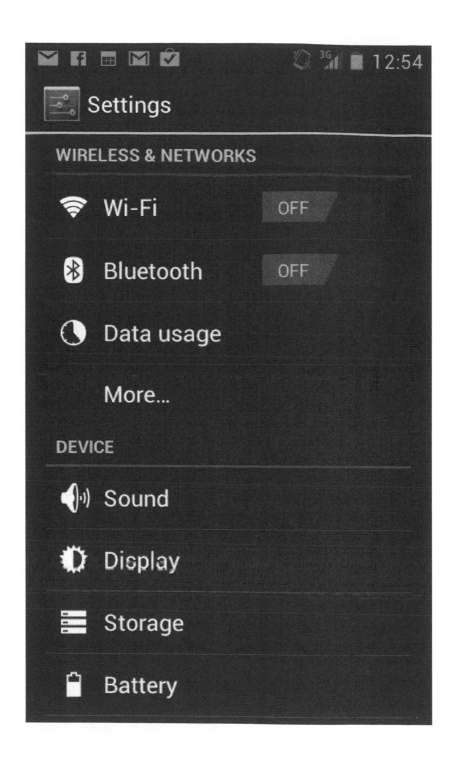

Chapter 9: Sync

One of the big conveniences of your Android smartphone is its ability to sync data with your various accounts. We've already discussed how to set those up earlier in the guide. However, keep in mind that all that syncing uses up battery life. You may want to change some account settings so it doesn't sync so often.

Here's how to configure general sync settings:

    ☐   Go to **Settings > Personal > Accounts & sync**.

    ☐   Check or uncheck the icon of the app you want to change to choose whether to auto-sync the app data.

If you turn off Auto-sync, you need to sync manually to collect updates for each app, and you won't receive notifications when updates occur.

If this option is not checked, you may be able to use an application's settings to sync data manually.

To manually sync data, just follow these steps:

Go to **Settings > Personal > Accounts & sync**.

    ☐   Touch name of the account you want to sync.

    ☐   Touch **Menu** icon

    ☐   Touch **Sync now**.

        To change an account's sync settings:

    ☐   Go to **Settings > Personal > Accounts & sync**.

☐ Touch the name of the account whose settings you want to change.

☐ You'll see the Sync Settings screen, with a list of the information that specific account syncs.

☐ Select the options you want to sync.

TIP: There are apps like Titanium Backup, MyBackup and ROM Manager that can backup a variety of data to help you recover if your phone is broken or stolen, or when you upgrade.

About Minute Help Press

Minute Help Press is building a library of books for people with only minutes to spare. Follow @minutehelp on Twitter to receive the latest information about free and paid publications from Minute Help Press, or visit minutehelp.com.

Printed in Great Britain
by Amazon.co.uk, Ltd.,
Marston Gate.